50
TRICKS
TO TEACH
YOUR DOG

50
TRICKS
TO TEACH
YOUR DOG

**Amaze your friends! Impress your family!
Challenge your dog!**

Sophie Collins

First published in 2010 by T.F.H. Publications
President/CEO Glen S. Axelrod
Executive Vice President Mark E. Johnson
Publisher Christopher T. Reggio
Production Manager Kathy Bontz
US Editor Stephanie Fornino
Cover Design Mary Ann Kahn

T.F.H. Publications, Inc. One TFH Plaza
Third and Union Avenues, Neptune City, NJ 07753 USA

ISBN: 978-0-7938-0645-4

Printed and bound in China
Color Origination by Ivy Press Reprographics.
10 11 12 13 14 1 3 5 7 9 8 6 4 2

Library of Congress Cataloging-in-Publication Data
Collins, Sophie.
   50 Tricks to Teach Your Dog / Sophie Collins
   0 p.cm.
   Includes Index.
   ISBN: 978-0-7938-0645-4 (alk paper)
   1. Tricks for Dogs. 1. Title. II. Title: 50 Tricks to Teach Your Dog
SF431.C625 2010
   636.7'0887--dc22
2010012064

This book was conceived, designed, and produced by
Ivy Press 210 High Street, Lewes, East Sussex BN7 2NS, UK
www.ivypress.co.uk

Creative Director Peter Bridgewater
Designer Clare Barber
Publisher Jason Hook
Photography Nick Ridley
Art Director Wayne Blades
Illustrator Joanna Kerr
Senior Editor Polita Anderson

The Leader in Responsible Animal Care for Over 50 Years!™
www.tfh.com

Contents

Introduction

Most dogs have a favorite game and most can perform at least one type of trick—even if it is just "Fetch." Maybe your dog loves playing this so much that you've never tried much else, or maybe he's a squeaky toy enthusiast who hasn't shown huge enthusiasm for other ideas he's been introduced to. But does this matter? Does he actually need a repertoire of different things to play at and learn to do?

The short answer is "yes." Your dog will benefit from learning to do different things and play a variety of games, and he'll get a lot out of the opportunity to interact with you, too. Dogs, along with humans, are one of comparatively few species of mammal that carry on playing into maturity, and there's evidence that they use play to learn and destress, as well as to engage with others. Plus, new games and tricks can help to keep boredom at bay—and dogs need to use their minds, as well as exercise their bodies, to stay happy and healthy.

Best of all, teaching your dog reinforces your role in his life as his mentor, the person through whom good things (rewards, fun, games) come, and the one he looks to for guidance in difficult situations. This last can be particularly useful if your dog tends toward independence and you'd prefer that he checked back with you more often than he does. If he's used to looking to you for his fun, he's more likely to look to you for help with something he isn't too sure about (unknown mailman, greeting a child, behaving nicely at a picnic) rather than just making his own mind up and depending purely on his own judgment. This is obviously a useful quality in the wild dog world, but less valuable in a domestic pet who's living with people.

A few points: Start and finish every session—whether trick training or playing a new game—practicing something you know your dog enjoys, so that even if he hasn't been successful in mastering something new, you're beginning and ending on a positive note. And be patient—some dogs are much quicker to pick up things than others. One pup may take six or eight sessions to master something that another may take weeks or even months to learn. However, even if you're not the owner of a canine Einstein, almost all dogs can learn a few simple tricks, provided that they're taught calmly and positively and are given plenty of time to absorb new things. Never push your dog beyond his frustration point. If he's getting fed up, you've been going on too long—make sure that you keep your play sessions fun for both of you.

Keep it Safe

The tricks and games that follow include some options for every kind of dog: small, large, young, or old. Even if your beloved pet is elderly or hasn't spent much time playing with you and learning new things, there'll still be some simple ideas you'll find that you can teach her. Do pay attention to the boxes on the pages—they offer safety advice when it's necessary and include some alternative suggestions for different elements for a game or trick to make it suitable for small or large breeds.

Pay attention to your dog when you're teaching active tricks. Usually, if a dog finds it physically uncomfortable to do a trick, she'll refuse to try it, so if she's normally eager to earn rewards and attention but is failing to engage with a particular game, it may not be the right trick for her. Never assume that your pet is being obstinate if she doesn't appear to want to do something, and never coerce her physically; not only is this ineffective, it may have the very undesirable side effect of making her scared of you or even of playing in general.

Jumping, in particular, should be taught carefully. Puppies shouldn't strain their joints while they are still growing, and elderly dogs who have back problems or who are stiff in the hips shouldn't jump or try any game that involves "crawling" on their bellies. Stick to some of the more mentally stimulating options if you have a dog who isn't very strong or agile physically.

And one last warning: Work with objects that are safe for your dog to play with. Toys manufactured specifically for dogs are the best options for hunt- or bring-the-object games. If you have a very "mouthy" dog who is strongly focused on mouthing and chewing any object that comes into her path, teach any collecting games with suitable props—nothing too small or that can be too easily chewed to pieces.

Once you have taken the safety advice into consideration, you can stop worrying and play wholeheartedly. You'll be rewarded with an enthusiastic pet who is thoroughly enjoying her dedicated time with you.

Working With Your Dog

If you've never made a habit of dedicated play-and-training sessions with your dog, it's worth thinking about his individual qualities before you begin—working with his strengths will get you the best results in whatever it is that you're teaching him.

What does he like to do? Does he love running and jumping best? If so, maybe you should start with something that is agility based. Is he the thoughtful type? He may thrive on some of the tougher working-it-out choices. What behavior do you want to encourage? It's surprising how many owners will teach their dog a game that involves jumping on the couch—and then complain when he jumps on the couch after the game is over. Be sure to play fair; only teach him things that you'll be happy for him to do when your play session is finished.

Think, too, about what your time together offers him. Almost every pet loves to spend time with his owner, but you should offer other payoffs, too. When he's starting to learn, if you find things going slowly, break a game or trick into plenty of steps and stages and reward even a tiny advance. Don't let the sesson go on for too long—five minutes at a time is plenty for a dog who's concentrating hard and trying to understand what it is that you want him to do. You don't want a turn to become boring; your pet must be enthusiastic about engaging with you and associate you with good things if you want to achieve positive results together.

Get used to encouraging him with your voice—and always use either an upbeat tone (for a dog who's heading in the right direction with the trick) or a low, calm "Uh-uh" if he's getting it wrong and needs to think again. Make sure that you keep your voice as positive as your attitude—dogs are finely attuned to tone and some are particularly noise sensitive. Don't hector him, and if you find that you're feeling frustrated yourself, don't raise your voice. Instead, consider whether it's time for the pair of you to take a short break and sit down together with a snack!

YAWN!!!

Saying What You Mean

When trainers and behaviorists assess dogs alongside their owners, one of their most frequent findings is that owners aren't saying what they think they are—or at least, not as far as the dog's concerned! It's hard for humans to remember that, however many words dogs pick up and however good they are at interpreting human intentions, they don't speak English—and most humans don't speak dog or even read its basics very well.

Whole books have been written on the subject of "reading" your dog and on telling her things in a language that she can understand (and they're worth hunting out if you have the time—some offer great insights) but here are a few basic tips that should help your pet to read what you're saying more clearly:

- Watch your body language. Are you moving involuntarily when you offer a verbal cue? One error owners frequently make without realizing is to lean toward their pet when they're asking her to come to them. To a dog, this reads as a mixed signal—and if you're not careful, it could become one of many.

- Don't loom. You'll read this again in some of the following games, but it bears saying more than once. Give your dog her own body space; she doesn't like someone much bigger than her leaning over and encroaching into her body space any more than you would.

- Watch your tone. We've already mentioned keeping it upbeat, but remember, too, to match your voice to the instruction you're giving. Sl-o-o-w, long, low noises will calm things down; happy, upbeat sounds will speed things up.

- Only say it once. This is the hardest thing of all for a human to master. Give your dog the chance to learn what a verbal cue means. Don't repeat it in a lot of variations "Come, come to me, good girl, that's it, COME HERE" sounds like a complicated configuration to a dog. If "Come" doesn't bring her running, then at the least try to repeat only what you said before, without making it any more complicated than it was the first time.

- If you use visual signals and verbal cues, make sure they always complement one another—don't mix and match and assume your dog will understand.

Clicker Training

USING A CLICKER

Clicker training has become immensely popular over the last decade. Many trainers use the clicker for teaching tricks because it can reinforce the behavior or action you want in your dog with very precise timing. The clicker is a small box with a metal tongue, which, when pressed with your thumb, makes a very clear "click." You first accustom your dog to listening for the click by clicking, then—immediately—giving him a treat. Once he's used to the idea that click equals treat, you can get specific with the behavior you want.

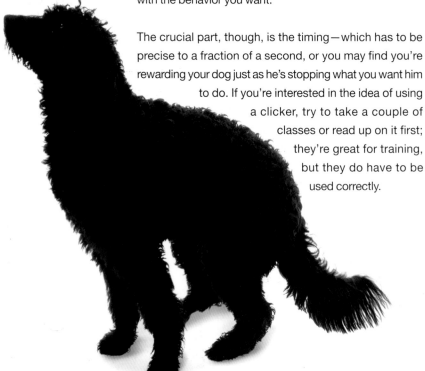

The crucial part, though, is the timing—which has to be precise to a fraction of a second, or you may find you're rewarding your dog just as he's stopping what you want him to do. If you're interested in the idea of using a clicker, try to take a couple of classes or read up on it first; they're great for training, but they do have to be used correctly.

Refreshing the Basics

Chances are that if you have an adult dog, he's already familiar with these three basics. But it may be that both of you could do with a refresher course before you move on to more complex games or tricks—if so, practice the following for a minute or two at the start of every play session.

SIT

Stand in front of your dog with a treat in your hand. Raise your hand; as his nose goes up to follow the treat, he'll automatically lower his bottom. Take your hand slightly over his head and, as he goes into a sit, give him the verbal cue "Sit" and give him the treat.

STAY

Put your dog in a sit, let him see that you're holding a treat, then back up a couple of paces, saying "Stay" as you do. If he starts to get up, ask him to sit again and, once again, back up. At first give him the treat for even a couple of seconds of "Stay"; as he gets used to it, you can try making him stay for slightly longer each time.

DOWN

Kneel facing your dog and ask him to sit. Holding a treat in your hand, slide it slowly forward in front of him, moving it a little farther as he leans forward to try to reach it. Say "Down" as he moves downward; as soon as he's fully lying down, give him the treat.

Simple Tricks

Whatever your dog's age, size, or intrinsic personality, you'll be able to teach him some of these little tricks. It's helpful if he already knows how to perform "Sit," "Down," and "Stay"; if he's rusty on these (or if he's simply never learned), take a look back at page 15 for a speedy refresher course. If you've never tried to teach your dog to do anything specific before, you'll find it easiest to start with something he loves to do anyway, so take note of his everyday behavior to see if he gives you any clues. Also, beginning with something simple means that he can enjoy some rapid success (and the treats and praise that go with it) and it will build his confidence for tougher options.

High Five

This repertoire basic is suitable for any size of dog and is usually simple to teach. If your dog is big, you can kneel in front of her and hold your hands at her natural paw level when you ask her to give you a "High five"; with a smaller dog you can sit cross-legged and lower your hands a little. You can also practice a "High five" from a standing position. Some dogs find it easier to start with a double-paw raise—technically a "High ten"—before balancing only one paw against your palm.

SAFETY When you're working with your pet face-to-face, remember that most dogs prefer not to make prolonged, direct eye contact, particularly with someone who's exactly at their eye level. A stare is rude and challenging in dog language, so don't stare at her as you teach this trick.

▶ ONE Ask your dog to sit down and, depending on her size, kneel or sit opposite her, or stand 1–2 feet (30–60cm) in front of her, so that you're face-to-face.

◀ TWO Holding up one of your hands, say "High five!" in an enthusiastic tone. Some dogs, eager for contact, will immediately raise a paw to meet your hand; others will need a touch on their paw or may even need you to lift it up slightly to get the idea. It's usually easier to teach this trick using praise rather than food treats, because most dogs will go for treats directly with their mouths and it can slow down the association they make with lifting their paws.

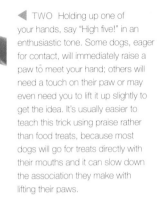

▶ THREE As soon as your dog is pawing at your hand, place your outstretched palm flat against it, supporting it in position, and praise your dog the instant she's holding the pose. If you want to try a "High ten," pat the other paw with your other hand, or, if your dog's happy to have her paws handled, pick it up and gently place it in position. The second that her paws are in place, praise her warmly, even if they're only there for an instant (you can build up to a slightly longer pose when she's got the idea). The dog here is shown in a begging "High ten" pose, sitting back on her hindquarters. Some dogs find it easier to balance while holding their paws up from this position than from a straight sit; encourage your dog to take whichever pose seems to come most naturally.

Left Paw, Right Paw

If your dog needs reminders to watch his manners when he's trying to attract your attention, or that of your visitors, teaching him to offer a specific paw for a "High five" will be a useful distraction—and instead of annoying people he'll charm them. You can use straightforward "Left paw" and "Right paw" cues to teach this one, but if you have a very "nosy" dog, you may have to remind him that he should be raising a paw to your hand rather than using his nose. Most dogs have a preferred paw that they'll always use first, so be sure to alternate the "right" and "left" cues in various different sequences while you're teaching to ensure that he learns to use both sides.

▼ ONE Ask your dog to sit and, depending on his size, kneel or sit opposite him, or stand 1–2 feet (30–60cm) in front of him, so that you're face to face. Using your right hand, tap his left foreleg, then raise your hand palm outward, saying "Left paw!" If necessary, pick his left paw up, holding it lightly in position against the palm of your right hand.

SHAKE HANDS

Some dogs find it much easier to lift their paws loosely than to hold a paw, pads out, to meet the palm of your hand. If you find a "High five" hard to teach your dog, try changing the instruction to "Shake hands" and add this to your dog's repertoire instead. You can come back to a "High five" later, but always end a teaching session with something your dog already knows how to do—even if it's a simple "Sit"— to make sure that you finish on a positive note.

◀ TWO As soon as the paw is in the right place, praise your dog warmly. Don't worry if he doesn't hold the pose for more than a moment at first; as he becomes used to the trick, he'll be happy to stay in position for longer.

▶ THREE Repeat the sequence, but this time using your left hand and his right paw. Again, praise him as soon as he holds his right paw in the pose, even if it's just for an instant. If he doesn't get it right, simply say "Uh-uh!" and try again. Most dogs will quickly get the idea and, after a few sessions of practice, will enjoy playing a game of "left paw, right paw" as you run through a sequence of lefts and rights in rapid succession.

▶ TWO When she's sitting, take a treat and hold it above and slightly behind her nose, saying "Say please!" as you do so. She'll tilt her head back so she can see it while simultaneously reaching up to get it. As she leans backward, her front paws will leave the floor and she'll balance back on her hindquarters.

▶ ONE "Say please" is easiest to teach with a food treat. Start by asking your dog to sit in front of you.

Say Please

This is the classic beg position, which you are probably familiar with from countless pictures of dogs. The begging pose comes very naturally to many smaller dogs; in general, though, the larger breeds are less enthusiastic about it and find it harder to balance upright on their hindquarters. If you have a big dog who's reluctant to beg, concentrate on a single-paw "High five" instead—she'll find it easier to hold the position without becoming uncomfortable.

SAFETY It's an oft-quoted experts' rule that you shouldn't teach a long-backed or elderly dog to beg. While it's definitely not a good idea to impose the trick on a senior dog or one that has back or hip problems, look out for what seems to come to your dog naturally. The little dachshund/spaniel cross shown in these pictures has a beautiful beg that she goes into very happily, despite having a long back. Usually, if your dog seems physically easy and happy with a position, it's safe for her to practice it.

▶ THREE As soon as she's balanced neatly, praise her and give her the treat. Don't ask her to hold the pose for more than a second or two at first, but as she becomes used to it, you can leave it a few moments longer before giving her the reward and releasing her.

Stand Up

This moves "Say please" another step forward—you ask your dog to stand on his hind legs and hold the pose for a moment or two. As with "Say please," this trick is generally more popular with smaller dogs, who are likely to find it easier to do. It's a good trick to teach a dog that tends to stand on his hind legs and paw you when you don't want him to. By teaching him to respond to a signal in this way, he'll gradually become conditioned to take up the behavior only when he hears the signal.

SAFETY It should go without saying that "Stand up," like "Say please," or any of the other games and tricks that call for a dog to spend some time balanced on only his back legs, aren't suitable to teach an old dog, or one that has any hip or back problems—it's too stressful for the joints and spine.

▶ ONE Ask your dog to sit down and stand facing him a little distance away.

◀ TWO When he's sitting comfortably, take a treat and hold it a little distance above and behind his nose. His natural response will be to begin to pull his body up to reach the treat, as he would for "Say please" on pages 22–23. As he rises up, say "Stand up!" in an encouraging voice and move the treat a little higher.

▶ THREE Instead of giving your dog the treat as he sinks back on his hindquarters, encourage him to stretch just a bit farther (you could try an upbeat "Hup" sound, too). As soon as he's standing completely on his back legs, give him the treat and praise him for his performance. Practice regularly until he can stand on his back legs easily without losing his balance.

BIG DOGS

||||||||||||||||||||||||||||||||||||||||||||||||||||||||||||||||||||||||||||||||||

If you have a big dog that tends to jump up and you want to link the jumping with a command (so that she only jumps when you encourage or let her), teach her "Take my arm" on pages 62–63 as an alternative to "Stand up"; it limits the height she "stands" at.

▶ ONE To walk confidently, your dog needs to be happy standing on her back legs, so before starting this trick make sure that your pet is relaxed about standing upright. When she's in an easy stand, continue to face her, treat in hand, held slightly above her nose level, and with a step or two's distance between you.

Walk Along

When your small dog is relaxed and standing at your request, see if you can teach her to walk on her back legs, too. If she's good at this trick, she's conquered one of the basic moves of doggy dancing, so you can both feel proud of yourselves. You may even want to consider broadening her performance skills by adding spinning around and jumping on command to great walking and you've got the basics of a nice routine!

◀ TWO Begin to move very slowly backward, increasing the distance between you slightly. As you do so, wave the treat and say "Walk along!" If her balance is good enough, she'll take a step or two forward to reach the treat. Give it to her and praise her as soon as she takes even a tiny, two-step "walk."

▶ THREE Gradually build the amount of time she can spend walking, leaving a second or so longer in each practice session before you give her the treat. Never continue to ask her to walk if she seems uncomfortable. Keep your practice sessions short and vary them with other kinds of games, so that she spends some of her time just running around on all fours!

27

Standing Ten

If a smaller dog isn't enthusiastic about performing a "High five" when balanced on his hindquarters, but is happy with standing up and walking along on his hind legs, try teaching him a "Standing ten" instead. Teach "Stand up" first, and don't try to extend it into a "Standing ten" until he's balancing comfortably on his back legs. Because you'll be using both your hands, this trick is easier to teach without using food treats. Since you're holding out your hands to meet your dog's paws, you may want to kneel in front of him—it's a better position from which to place your hands flat against his pads and, if necessary, to support him while he's still learning.

▼ TWO Ask him to "Stand up," adding an enthusiastic "Hup" sound if it helps him to get the message.

▶ ONE Kneel in front of your dog, facing him, leaving about 1 foot (30cm) of space between you. Ask him to sit.

▼ THREE The moment that he's standing on his hind legs, hold out your hands, palms forward, and say "Standing ten!" You can support him if he needs help in balancing, but try to get his paws placed pads out on your hands before he drops down again. Praise him warmly as soon as he's holding the pose, even if it's just for a second or two.

◀ ONE Get your dog's attention. As soon as she's focused on you, hold a treat above her nose and slowly begin to move your hand in a large circle a little above her head.

Spin Around

H ere is another building block toward a doggy dance routine. In this move, your dog turns in a neat circle, following a circling motion of your hand and a verbal reminder. It can be taught entirely by using a treat as a lure, but don't forget to use the verbal cue "Spin around," too, or it may take longer for your dog to learn to take a spin without a food bribe. If your dog is one of many who spins around naturally whenever she gets excited, you can reinforce the move by saying "Spin around" and treating her whenever she starts to turn in a circle.

▲ TWO She'll follow your hand, and as she does so, say "Spin around!," continuing to move your hand around as you do so.

TEACHING TIP

|||||||||||||||||||||||||||||||||||||||||||||||||||||||||||||||||||||||||||||||||||||||||||||||||||||||||||

When you're teaching your dog something completely new, don't stint on either treats or praise—plenty of both will help her to get the idea and keep her enthusiastic. As she learns more, praise her whenever she gets it right, but make the treats a bit more random—rewarding her every few successful attempts, but not every time. When you give food rewards, choose something she really loves; that way, she'll learn it's always worthwhile paying attention to you.

◀ THREE As she takes a full turn, praise your dog and, as she completes the full spin, give her the treat.

▶ FOUR Repeat once or twice, encouraging your dog to turn the full circle before giving the treat, then try once or twice more, picking up speed and using the same cue but holding your finger out for your dog to follow rather than a treat. If you practice regularly, she'll soon be spinning in neat circles as soon as you ask her to.

Off to Bed

It's useful if your dog understands that sometimes he should settle down in his own space for a while. Most dogs will have a favorite quiet spot or two at home—places they'll go when they want some peace or a little downtime. If you want him out from underfoot, teach him that "Off to bed" indicates that he should go somewhere specific. It helps, at least at first, if you use it only to refer to a single place or object (perhaps his basket or crate or his own towel or rug), rather than as a generic cue to sit down and stay quiet.

SEIZE THE MOMENT

This behavior is easy to teach opportunistically—wait until your dog is on his way to lie down in "his" spot, then tell him, as he sets off, "Off to bed" and praise him when he lies down. This reinforces those times when he isn't so eager for a break but you want him to take one anyway!

▲ ONE Choose the place where you want your pet to go to bed with care. It should be somewhere he already likes to settle down. Wait until a time when he would usually be headed for a rest anyway—after a long walk or play session, perhaps, or when he's about to go off for an evening doze. Then indicate his space by looking toward it and say "Off to bed!" If he looks at you for more clues, pat the blanket, basket, or whatever you are using and repeat the direction.

◀ TWO Few dogs need much more encouragement than this when they're already tired and ready for a break. Your dog will probably go over to his space and settle down right away.

◀ THREE If he's slow to head for "his" place, walk over toward it and call him over, then kneel down and encourage him to settle. As he lies down, praise and treat him, then leave him alone. After a few practice runs, he'll understand that "Off to bed" means quiet time.

Learning a "Stop" Signal

This trick will help you to get your dog to quiet down quickly when you need her to settle. An exuberant pet needs to learn that playtime stops when you say so. Your dog may find it hard to wind down after she's become worked up during a play session, so if you can learn to calm her down fast when you need to, it'll prove invaluable both at home and when you're out and about together. Remember that your tone of voice is very important in helping you to control your dog—use a happy, higher-pitched and upbeat tone when you want to raise your dog's levels of stimulation and a calm, quiet, level tone when you want to lower them. Never shout—it may be an effective way to catch her attention but it won't be helpful in getting her to obey you.

SMALL DOGS

No one wants a pesty pet, but small dogs are often allowed to get away with more in terms of behavior—purely because their size means they're less intrusive than bigger dogs when they act up. If you have a small dog, don't let her develop a Napoleon complex: teach her a "Stop" sign (plus the "Off to bed" cue) and you'll be helping to ensure that she's welcome everywhere she goes.

▲ ONE Here's the situation: Playtime is over, but your dog is still leaping around after her toy and ignoring you. If you try to take her toy away, she reads it as a sign that you're getting ready to play again. What should you do? Stay calm and stop chasing around after her. Instead, stand still and, using a low voice, say "Stop!" in an authoritative tone, at the same time holding out a hand tilted toward the floor.

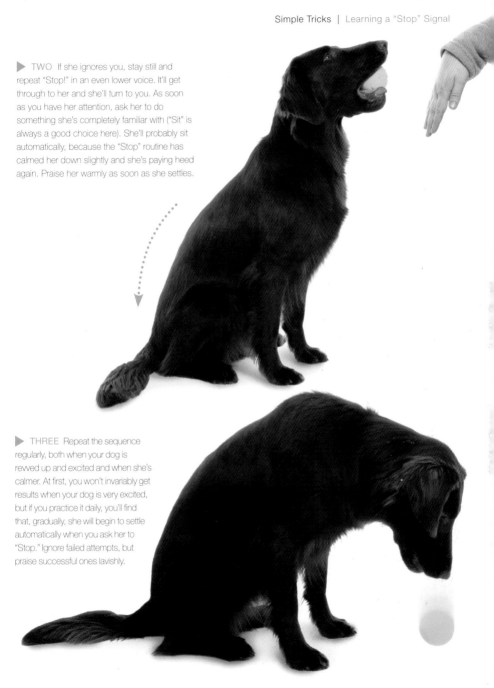

▶ TWO If she ignores you, stay still and repeat "Stop!" in an even lower voice. It'll get through to her and she'll turn to you. As soon as you have her attention, ask her to do something she's completely familiar with ("Sit" is always a good choice here). She'll probably sit automatically, because the "Stop" routine has calmed her down slightly and she's paying heed again. Praise her warmly as soon as she settles.

▶ THREE Repeat the sequence regularly, both when your dog is revved up and excited and when she's calmer. At first, you won't invariably get results when your dog is very excited, but if you practice it daily, you'll find that, gradually, she will begin to settle automatically when you ask her to "Stop." Ignore failed attempts, but praise successful ones lavishly.

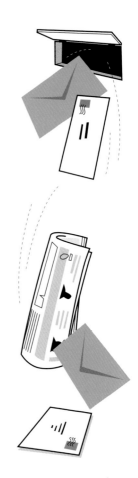

Answer the Door

Most dogs love to answer the door, and sometimes their excited barking and jumping can be almost uncontrollable. If you teach your dog to bark on request when someone arrives at the door, however, you'll find that it's also easier to stop him from being noisy, because he's learned the barking as a behavior he performs when you ask him to, rather than a reflex action that he does purely because he wants to.

▲ ONE If your dog already barks when someone comes to the door, look out for the exact moment at which he begins and, as he does so, tell him to "Answer the door!" Speak in the upbeat tone you use for positive instruction; he'll be happy to continue to bark! If, on the other hand, you own one of the rare dogs that doesn't bark to alert you to visitors, you'll have to wait until he starts to bark in some other context, perhaps during an exciting game.

TWO Once your dog is barking, run to the door with him (if he isn't already there), then stop the barking using your downward hand signal and a serious, low-voiced "Stop" as described on pages 34–35. It will take a little practice to get your dog barking on demand and stopping when you ask, but it's worth mastering because it means that you won't have a problem with constant, annoying barking at other times. Practice consistently and regularly—daily if you can.

THREE Sometimes you'll find it works well to ask your dog to do something else as soon as he stops barking—this will distract him from starting again. Suggest something easy that he already knows—"Sit" or "Lie down" are good options.

Rainy Day Tricks

Your dog's bouncing with energy but it's raining too hard to take her out for a long walk, and you can't stand her theatrical canine sighing anymore. What should you do? This chapter has some ideas to keep you both occupied and out of trouble, even when you have to stay indoors. Whether you pick the dog-friendly "Pan of Treats," the crowd-pleasing "Are You Ashamed of Yourself?," or even the hilarious bubble-chasing game, there'll be something here to keep you both happily occupied until the sun comes out again.

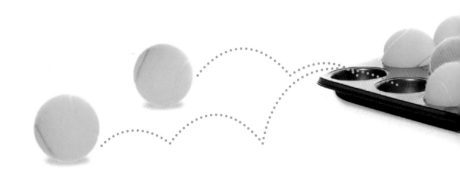

Pan of Treats

This is simple to set up and a lot of fun for your dog. Your pet needs to lift the tennis ball right out of the muffin pan holes because they are too deep to let the ball simply to be pushed to one side. It doesn't need much, if any, teaching and most pets will quickly grasp the idea; however, if your dog is slow to pick it up, show him how to play by lifting out one or two balls yourself to reveal the treats underneath. The only dogs it isn't suitable for are those who are more interested in playing ball than in treats—in which case, you may find that your dog races into another room with a tennis ball and tries to tempt you into something more energetic!

SMALL DOGS

||||||||||||||||||||||||||||||||||||||||||||||||

Tennis balls may be too hefty for tiny toy breeds to lift. If your pet fits into this category, hunt out a pan with small holes (a mini-muffin pan will work well provided that the holes aren't too deep) and smaller, lighter balls. Even the teeniest chihuahua should be able to manage a table tennis ball.

◀ ONE Take a muffin pan and as many tennis balls (or other balls of equivalent size) as you can gather together. Put one of your dog's favorite treats in each of the holes in the muffin pan, then place a tennis ball over the treat.

TWO Put the pan on the floor and lift one of the balls briefly to show your dog the treat underneath. Then push the pan toward him and let him go. He may try to push the tennis balls aside as first, but he'll soon get the hang of picking them up.

THREE Once he's earned one or two treats by taking the balls out of the pan, he'll become eager in his search for more. And as he gets more accomplished in emptying the pan, you can try a round or two against the clock. Keep the treats small, though—you don't want him to pile on the pounds. And don't forget to wash the pan thoroughly before your next baking project!

◀ ONE Put your dog into a sit/ stay position, and make sure she watches while you put a treat under the mat. Put it just under the edge at first so that it's easy for her to get.

Are You Ashamed of Yourself?

This is an excellent trick for when you have company. Practice it until your pet is really proficient before putting on a performance in front of visitors—it's certain to win your clever canine a round of applause. Pick a rug or mat that's a good weight for her to push up with her nose—this might be something light, such as a bath mat, or, for a large dog, such as a German Shepherd, something a little heavier, like the edge of a rug or carpet runner. She should be able to pucker up the edge easily.

◀ TWO In an excited tone, say "Are you ashamed of yourself?" and tap the edge of the mat with your hand. She'll start to push her nose under to hunt out the treat, puckering up the mat as she does. As she gets her nose under the edge, praise her.

▲ THREE If she's too quick to grab the treat without getting into the position you want, keep your hand under the edge of the mat and hold the treat in it. Give it to her only when her nose is right under the edge. When she's reliably pushing her nose under the mat, try using the command without the treat. Practice regularly and she'll soon be getting into the right position on the command.

BIG DOGS

Some larger dogs are less comfortable putting their heads right down on the floor to do this trick. If so, put the treat under a rug or cushion placed on a chair instead—your dog may be happier to perform when training involves her practicing a trick at face level.

Take It

This is a great building block to all kinds of tricks and games. You're teaching your dog to take something in his mouth—either from your hand or (usually at the next stage) to pick it up from the floor. It comes completely naturally to some dogs, while others take a little time to learn it. You'll find it easiest to practice with something your dog already loves to play with. You won't have too much trouble teaching a ball enthusiast to "take" a tennis ball, for example. And suit the prop to the dog: retrieving types may enjoy taking a plushy toy; more "chewy" breeds might prefer something harder, with more resistance to it.

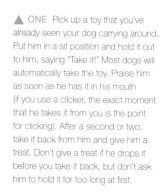

▲ ONE Pick up a toy that you've already seen your dog carrying around. Put him in a sit position and hold it out to him, saying "Take it!" Most dogs will automatically take the toy. Praise him as soon as he has it in his mouth (if you use a clicker, the exact moment that he takes it from you is the point for clicking). After a second or two, take it back from him and give him a treat. Don't give a treat if he drops it before you take it back, but don't ask him to hold it for too long at first.

◄ TWO When your dog has become used to taking a toy from your hand and holding it himself, try "Take it" with the same toy lying nearby on the floor.

THREE Keep it very near for the first few attempts, and look at the toy as you say the cue. Again, praise (and, if you're using a clicker, click) immediately when he picks it up—make sure that your timing is exact, so that he knows exactly what he's getting the praise for. Gradually, you can wait a moment or two longer to praise as he picks up the toy more easily. Once he's got the idea, use the instruction with different toys, so that your dog associates the cue with the action rather than the toy and gets used to picking up different things.

FOUR When your dog is picking up various toys with ease, you can make the cue the starting point of a game—ask him to "Take it," then run outside with him carrying the toy and play a game with him. It'll make him even eager to do as you ask.

Dinner Time

What could be cuter than a dog who brings you her dinner bowl when she's hungry? The only prop you need is a bowl that's light enough for your dog to carry easily, a dog that knows the "Take it" command and is also happy to bring things to you. As she gets more confident in bringing the bowl, you'll be able to ask your dog to take it to visitors, too—just suggest that they ask her if it's her dinner time yet.

▼ ONE This trick has two parts: first the dog needs to pick up her bowl and then she must come to you and hand it over. Start by getting her to pick it up. Place the bowl on the floor close to you and your dog, and ask her to "Take it." Praise her when she takes it and holds it in her mouth.

SAFETY Only use light, plastic bowls for this trick. Dogs don't usually like to pick up metal objects in their mouths and it's not sensible to ask a dog to run around with a ceramic bowl, so play it safe with the plastic option.

▲ TWO As soon as she's picking up the bowl enthusiastically, ask her to bring it to you. If she already knows a "Fetch" command, use that; if not, get her attention and ask her to "Fetch" or "Bring it," using an enthusiastic voice and body language. Use a treat as a lure if you find it helpful.

▶ THREE When she brings the bowl to you, say "Dinner time!" and praise her warmly as you take it from her (or exchange it for a treat). If you practice regularly, your dog will gradually cut out the interim steps when she sees the bowl, and she'll learn to bring it straight to you when she hears the "Dinner time" cue.

Lion Tamer

Choose a small, low piece of furniture with a nonslip top for this trick. Your dog will leap onto it, then sit, neatly posed, in a "Stay" position—like a lion perching on a stool in an old-fashioned circus. Very small breeds can even be encouraged to go into a begging position, rather than simply sitting. If your dog's an enthusiastic jumper, he'll learn this one easily. Make sure you choose a piece of furniture that he's allowed to treat as "his"; you should be consistent about where your dog is allowed to sit, so don't let him do something as part of a trick or game that he isn't allowed to do normally.

SMALL DOGS

If you can train your small dog to stay standing on a stool or ottoman when he's jumped, you've made a great start to a grooming session, because he'll be at a convenient level for you to give him an overall brushing and combing. Use the "Jump" command, give him a treat, then ask him to stay.

▶ ONE Place the stool or ottoman in a clear area on the floor so that your dog has plenty of jumping space. Pat the top with your hand and say "Hup!" Most dogs will take the cue right away; if yours isn't sure, gently pick him up and place him in position once or twice, giving him a treat when he's in a pose.

◀ TWO Standing is the best position if you're planning a grooming session (see box left). However, if you simply want your dog to pose nicely, wait until he's standing on the ottoman, then ask him to sit.

▶ THREE Ask your dog to stay for a moment or two, praise him, and then release him. Most dogs like to be high up—they can see what's going on around them better. If you place "his" lion tamer's stool near a window, you may find that he elects to use it as a regular perch to sit and watch the world go by.

SAFETY Encourage your dog to jump onto only nonslip surfaces. Those covered in upholstery or fabric are fine, but a varnished or wooden surface isn't a good idea—his paws may not be able to find a grip and he may fall.

Chasing Bubbles

Less a trick than an activity, bubble chasing can be an effective way to use up a bit of excess canine energy on a rainy day. Dogs are often simply amazed by bubbles, and you'll love the surprised expression on your pet's face as she finally gets right up to her elusive prey—only to have it go "pop" on the end of her nose. You can use a child's bubble-blowing set or even a wand with a strong soap mixture to blow the bubbles with. Start gently, blowing a small string of bubbles close to your dog; then, when you've caught her attention, try sending them around the room or blowing them in front of an electric fan to get her jumping around after them.

AIR FARE

If your dog becomes a serious bubble enthusiast, you can indulge her by buying some of the commercial just-for-dogs bubble options—you can find bacon- or chicken-scented bubble mixes online or in large pet stores—plus machines that will even do the bubble blowing for you.

Cross My Paws

This elegant posture seems to come easily to some of the larger breeds—owners of greyhounds and labradors will often find them adopting the languid, cross-paw "relaxing" pose naturally. If this is true of your dog, all you need to do is to praise and give him a treat when you see your dog settle down and cross his paws. If it isn't something your dog does of his own accord, he may need a little help.

 ONE Wait until your dog has settled down and is lying in a relaxed pose. This is a good trick to practice when he's already had some exercise; otherwise, you may find that he jumps at the chance of interacting with you and leaps up, ready to play, as soon as you pay some attention to him.

▶ TWO Kneel down beside him, gently take hold of one of his paws, and lay it over the other. As you do so, say "Cross your paws!" enthusiastically. The instant his paws are in the right position, praise the dog and give him a treat.

▼ THREE Sit back on your heels and see if he holds the position. If he unfolds his paws, place them back in the crossed position. If he stays still, you can reinforce the pose with a "Good dog!" Some dogs may paw at you as you leave their paws crossed. If yours is one of them, you can convert the raised paw into a handshake to finish off the trick.

Under the Bridge

I n "Under the bridge," you're teaching your dog to crawl under the "bridge" of your raised knees as you sit on the floor. This is easiest to teach if you lure your dog with her favorite food treat. Small dogs will find it easier than larger breeds (they have more space to go through!) but most medium-size dogs will also be happy to make the moves if you have a really delicious lure to tempt them through. If your dog really is too big for the space under your knees, teach the alternative option (see box below).

▼ ONE Sit on the floor with your knees raised, leaving a gap under your legs. Call your dog to you and ask her to sit at one side of you.

BIG DOGS

If you have a really big dog, she won't be able to fit under your knees for this trick. Instead, find a space that's big enough for her to wriggle through with a little effort, perhaps under a hurdle bar set at the right height. Lure her through, holding a treat on the other side of the bar.

TWO Take a treat in the hand opposite to your dog and hold your hand down at floor level on the opposite side from your dog. She'll lower her head and sniff at the treat; as she does, pull it slightly farther away from the bridge made by your raised knees. Your dog will follow the treat through; say "Through!" as she does. As soon as she goes completely through the gap, give her the treat and praise her.

THREE After a few tries, when your dog's following the lure with ease, try the trick again, but treat your dog only every second or third successful attempt. Don't stint on the verbal praise, though. After a little more practice, you'll find that you can fold your hands out of the way, and your dog will go under the bridge on just the "Through" command.

Commando Crawl

If you've already taught your dog to go "Under the bridge" (see pages 54–55), then he'll have some idea of the crawling action this sneaky-looking move calls for. He will need to be lying down but in the ready-to-go position before you start—if he's in a relaxed down with both his legs under him but to one side, he won't be in a good pose for crawling. It's best, too, to teach this trick on a soft, carpeted surface; most dogs will be happier to crawl on a surface that isn't too slippery or chilly.

▼ ONE Ask your dog to lie down, but start on the trick while he's still in an alert position—that is, before he switches into a completely relaxed position with his hindquarters lying over on one side. Have two or three food treats in your hand—you'll probably need more than one to encourage your dog to get a good crawl motion.

▼ TWO Hold a food treat 3–4 inches (7.5–10cm) up from the ground, between finger and thumb, just out of your dog's reach. If he starts to get up, say "Uh-uh!" and ask him to lie down again.

▼ THREE Gradually move the treat away from his nose, keeping it at the same height from the floor (if you hold it at floor level, he'll try to push his nose under your hand to get the treat; if it's slightly raised from the floor, you'll be encouraging the crawl more effectively). As he creeps forward, praise him effusively and give him the treat.

SAFETY Don't teach this trick to an elderly dog, one with a very long back, or one who has any history of back or hip trouble—the creeping movement may aggravate an existing problem.

▼ FOUR Put another treat in your hand and lure your dog forward again. Stay aware of the height the treat is at, and the position it's luring your dog into. As he crawls just a little more, reward him again. This is a difficult pose for a dog to hold, so plentiful rewards and brief practice sessions are best. Don't go on too long; you don't want to strain his joints.

Back Up

This is one of those useful commands that can stop your pet in her tracks when she's making a nuisance of herself. When you're teaching "Back up," remain very aware of your own body language and tone of voice. It's important to relay the message in your manner as well as in the verbal cue you're offering.

▶ ONE There's a time and a place for everything, so if your dog is leaping about energetically and paying no attention to you, here's a way to calm her down.

MIND YOUR LANGUAGE!

When you're calming your dog down and trying to focus her on you, use an authoritative tone and, when it's appropriate, a clear hand signal. Stand well back and and don't loom into her body space, particularly if she is a small dog, because she may find this threatening and that won't help her to concentrate on what you want her to do.

▶ TWO Hold up your hand, using the signal shown, and say "Back up!" in a clear, calm voice. Say it just once; if you time it right, speaking into a quiet moment, your dog will stop what she's doing and turn her attention on you. Move toward her slightly as you speak.

Just the
Two of You

You and your dog already love spending time together, and this section concentrates on some tricks and games that will enhance your closeness. They call on him to pay close attention to what you're teaching him, and you and your possessions act as props to the trick in many of them. Whether you want to walk arm-in-arm with your larger dog (one that you'll want to encourage in only large breeds!) or to teach your pet to carry your bag or collect your keys before you go out together, you'll learn how to here. Plus you can find out how to teach your dog to hunt for you or chase you—both are good games for dogs that can seem a little too independent-minded for their own good!

Take My Arm

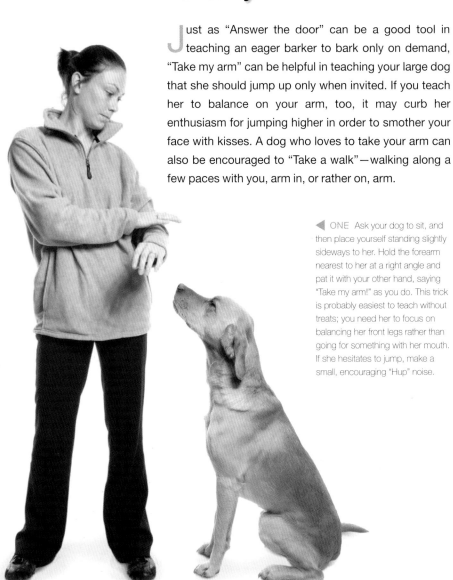

Just as "Answer the door" can be a good tool in teaching an eager barker to bark only on demand, "Take my arm" can be helpful in teaching your large dog that she should jump up only when invited. If you teach her to balance on your arm, too, it may curb her enthusiasm for jumping higher in order to smother your face with kisses. A dog who loves to take your arm can also be encouraged to "Take a walk"—walking along a few paces with you, arm in, or rather on, arm.

◀ ONE Ask your dog to sit, and then place yourself standing slightly sideways to her. Hold the forearm nearest to her at a right angle and pat it with your other hand, saying "Take my arm!" as you do. This trick is probably easiest to teach without treats; you need her to focus on balancing her front legs rather than going for something with her mouth. If she hesitates to jump, make a small, encouraging "Hup" noise.

SMALL DOGS

This isn't a trick for a small dog, even if she's an enthusiastic jumper. You can teach a variation to small breeds if you kneel or sit alongside them, with your arm angled in the same way. Don't be surprised, however, if a dog who loves to jump suddenly vaults high enough to give you a sloppy kiss when you're in such tempting proximity.

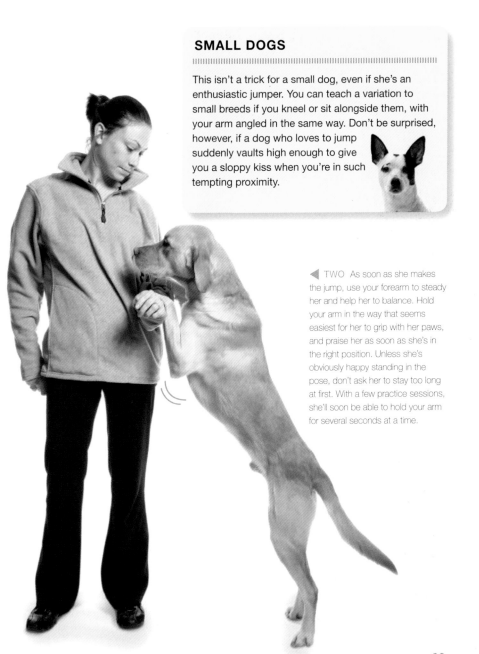

◀ TWO As soon as she makes the jump, use your forearm to steady her and help her to balance. Hold your arm in the way that seems easiest for her to grip with her paws, and praise her as soon as she's in the right position. Unless she's obviously happy standing in the pose, don't ask her to stay too long at first. With a few practice sessions, she'll soon be able to hold your arm for several seconds at a time.

Catch the Owner

While any game that encourages your dog to run away from you is a bad idea, enticing your dog to chase you as you run away from *him* is a great way to show him that he's the one who has to keep up with you, not the other way around. Both this and "Come find" on pages 68–69 are useful if your dog's attention is prone to wander away from you. If you can make every time he comes to you into an enjoyable game, you're far more likely to be successful in the future when you're calling him away from something he wants to carry on doing. Plus it's good exercise for you, too.

▲ ONE This is best played outside—you won't be able to get far enough away from your dog indoors to start a chase. Wait until your dog is paying attention to something else and is already at a little distance from you. Don't try it for the first time when he's doing something distracting (such as playing with his best dog friend)—eventually, you'll be able to get him to chase after you every time, but it will take some practice.

TEACHING TIP

If you can't run fast enough to give your dog a stimulating chase, enlist a friend to stand some distance away and take turns calling your dog. Most dogs will love racing between two people, getting praise and attention from both.

▶ TWO Start to run in the opposite direction from your dog. As you run, call to him in an excited voice, making plenty of upbeat noise—you can add whistling and hand claps if you want to. You can look over your shoulder to see if he's coming, but don't stop—keep running as fast as you can.

▼ THREE Dogs love to chase: As soon as he notices that you're initiating a game that he's more used to playing with other dogs, he'll eagerly race after you. Praise and make a fuss of him when he catches up—then run away again. Without the advantage of surprise, he's bound to catch up with you faster the second time around!

Walk Around

This is a development from spinning in a circle, but instead of chasing her tail, your dog does her turn with you in the center of the turning ring instead. This is a popular doggy dancing staple; if you find that your pet's an eager performer, you could practice turning circles together to music—she's likely to be particularly enthusiastic if she feels that you're joining in, too. If your dog can follow a mark, you can try this trick without treats by asking her to follow your finger; however, if not, it's easy to teach using small food treats as a lure.

▲ ONE Begin by calling your dog to you: First get her attention, then, either holding a treat between two fingers or using a downward finger as a mark for her, begin to trace a circle around the front of your body, saying "Walk around!" as you start.

TWO As she begins to follow, take your hand around the side of your body. Keep the hand with the treat in it close to your legs so that the circle she is being brought in is neat and tight.

THREE Bring your hand as far behind your legs as you can, then quickly either switch the treat to your other hand (so you don't have to turn around yourself) or, if you're pointing, swap the hand you use to point with.

FOUR Wait until she's walked the full circle, then praise her and give her a treat.

Come Find

Like "Catch the owner," this is a good game to play if your dog seems inclined to take your constant presence for granted. It's easiest to play outside (which offers a larger, more unfamiliar space and more things that you can hide behind) but, when the weather's bad, you can try it indoors instead. Swap the places you hide around and don't rule out the really unexpected; in fact, apply the same rules as you would playing with people — your dog will be amazed and thrilled to finally locate you in a closet, for instance! And it's good training for your dog to learn that it's worth keeping an eye out for you, whatever other distractions are going on.

TEACHING TIP

You can usually play this game only once every day or two, because after one round your dog will stay by your side, waiting for the next thing to happen. However, it's a good way to start off a training session, because he'll end it in an attentive mindset, ready to learn something new.

▶ ONE Wait until your dog is slightly distracted (only slightly—five minutes after you've presented him with a new marrow bone is not the moment to try this game), then hide from him. Ideally, pick somewhere unexpected, at least a couple of rooms away; don't make it too easy.

▶ TWO Call your dog to you, or whistle, or even use the click of a clicker. Your dog will be alert and start looking for you. If he's taking longer than expected, make the noise again, but don't keep calling him—remember, it's his job to track you down, and he's already got the built-in advantage of a sharp sense of smell.

▶ THREE When he eventually finds you—in the closet, behind the couch, under a table—make a big fuss of him.

Follow the Target

It's useful to teach your dog to mark a target with her nose, because her ability to do this can be the building block to more complex tricks—for example, you can use this to teach her to close a door for herself. This exercise is simple and shows you how to teach your dog to "follow" your hand or finger with her nose. The aim is to get her to "mark" your hand with her nose.

▼ ONE Ask your dog to sit down in front of you. Stand or kneel in front of her, put a small treat between the base of two of the fingers of your right hand, then hold it out to her, palm outward. Say "Target!" as you do so.

BIG AND SMALL DOGS

With a big dog, teach "Follow the target" from a standing position, but keep your hand down low at the level of her nose and ask her to sit, as you would a smaller breed, before you start. With a tiny or toy dog, get right down to her level, sitting on the ground, to get your hand level with her nose, and also ensure that she sits before you start.

◀ TWO She'll automatically begin to nose at your hand to try to get the treat. As her nose makes contact with your palm, say "Target!" again and give her the treat. Repeat this once or twice, alternating hands, until she's moving her nose directly to your palm, whichever hand you choose to use.

◀ THREE When she's got the idea, hold your hand out to her, palm out, but without a treat between the fingers, using "Target" as the cue again. When she touches your hand with her nose, give her a treat, but from the other hand. After a few repeats only give her a treat once every two or three times she gets it right. When she's invariably marking your palm, try giving a visual cue by holding out a single finger—eventually, she'll be able to "mark" this, too.

▶ ONE Stand to one side of your dog, so that you're both facing the same way. Ask him to sit down alongside you. You may find that you (or your dog) are naturally right- or left-sided; pick whichever side is most comfortable for you both. Have a handful of small treats ready.

Look Left, Look Right, and Cross the Road

This is a cute trick for when you're out and about together—plenty of dogs have learned to sit obediently at the curb until you tell them it's time to cross, but far fewer have learned to check the traffic flow by looking left and right in the same way that you do. You'll raise a laugh from other pedestrians when your dog shows off his savvy before you cross together. Make sure that he's getting it perfect every time before you show it off to strangers.

TEACHING TIP

||||||||||||||||||||||||||||||||||||||||||||||

Although it can be tempting to practice this trick while keeping your dog on the leash (after all, he'll be restrained when you're out and about), it's better if he learns it off the leash; you want him to follow what you say rather than "help" him with the movements of the leash; it's best for you to rely on your voice to direct him.

◀ TWO Say "Look left!," at the same time holding a treat well off on his left hand side. He'll turn his head, and as he does so, praise him and give him a treat. Repeat on the other side, saying "Look right!," and holding the treat well off to his right side. Again, he'll turn to look at it; again, praise him and give him a treat as he does. Repeat this several times, alternating sides. As soon as he's clearly associating the head turn with the verbal cue, cut down the treats, offering one only every second or third successful attempt.

▶ THREE Now that he's looking left and right, it's time to "Cross the road." Go through steps one and two, then walk forward, saying "And ... cross the road!" enthusiastically as you do. Practice the whole sequence over several sessions until he's cue perfect, then take him out to show off in public how smart he is.

▶ ONE Wait until it's nearly time to go out and your dog is getting excited about her forthcoming walk. Place the leash somewhere where it's easily accessible to her (on the floor, or on a low chair or table), then get her attention, indicate the leash, and ask her to "Take it."

Walk Yourself

Many dogs love to hold something in their mouths when they're out for a walk—and you can teach your dog to carry her leash when you're not holding the other end of it. A woven fabric or tape leash is the best kind to use for this; it's easier for her to pick up and carry than the heavier chain or thick leather kind. It's best to teach the "Take it" instruction on pages 44–45 before you start on "Walk yourself," and also to practice this around the house and yard before you ask her to carry her leash on a walk; you want to be sure that she's not prone to drop it before you go out.

SMALL DOGS

If you're teaching this trick to a very small dog, make sure that the leash is light enough and is knotted to make it small enough for her to be able to carry easily. A large, heavy leash may discourage her from carrying it very far.

▶ TWO Praise her when she picks it up. If it's trailing and she seems to be finding it awkward to carry, knot it up a little to make it easier for her. Now ask her to "Come along" and walk briskly away. She'll probably follow you, and if you don't take the leash she's likely to keep carrying it. If she drops it, ask her to "Take it" again and wait until she picks it up before walking on.

▼ THREE After a few sessions, you should be able to ask her to carry her leash whenever you're out somewhere where it's safe for her to do so. Make sure she understands that when she's "Walking herself," she's also accompanying you— when it's time for off-the-leash play, reclaim the leash so it doesn't get lost.

Carry My Bag

If your dog has learned to carry his leash, you can try extending the trick and asking him to take one of your bags for you. Pick a soft, washable bag—a fabric tote is ideal for larger breeds, but you may have to find something much smaller if you have a little dog. It's a good idea to put one or two light items in it before you start (you could include a package of treats or a favorite toy for rewarding him after he's been carrying the bag for a while). Knot the handles if it will make it easier for your pet to carry.

◀ ONE As with "Walk yourself" on pages 74–75, start by placing the bag somewhere accessible and obvious. Stand at the other end of the room and ask your dog to "Take it." If your dog starts to rummage about with the contents, however, discourage him with a firm "Uh-uh." As soon as he picks it up, praise him and call him to you.

◀ TWO He may be somewhat tentative about carrying something with some weight. If he hesitates or puts the bag down, ask him to "Take it" again, and call him to you right away.

◀ THREE As soon as he gets it into his head that he needs to come to you with the bag, he's got the basic idea of the trick. Even if he's only carried it across the room, make a big fuss of him and look in the bag for a toy or a treat to reward him. Then practice regularly, increasing the distance between you. When your dog can bring you the bag from another room in the house, you can try the trick when out shopping. You can even ask him to hold your bag while you're getting out your purse to pay!

▲ ONE Stand with your back to your dog, and attract her attention by bending down and making smooching noises to her. Hold a treat down between your knees so that she can see it.

Peekaboo

In this trick, your dog walks between your legs from behind, then sits down, peeping out from between your knees. A dog will only place herself in this vulnerable position with someone she really trusts, so unless she's one of those rare pets who adores everyone she meets, don't expect her to perform this trick with anyone but you. This is a good choice if you have a natural performer; she'll look so cute peering out that she's certain to get a lot of laughter and praise from onlookers.

SMALL DOGS

A very small dog may hesitate before walking between your legs like this—if she seems nervous, try to make it less intimidating for her by kneeling instead, so that you're closer to her level, then lure her through with a treat just as you would if you were standing.

 TWO As soon as she's positioned directly behind you, pull your hand forward to encourage her to walk between your legs, saying "Peekaboo!" as you do.

▶ THREE As she reaches the midpoint, ask her to sit, then praise her and give her a treat as soon as she does. Encourage her to sit for a few seconds before getting up again.

Fetch My Keys

Because a bunch of keys is small, hard, and metallic, it is usually harder to succeed in getting your dog to pick it up than it would be something softer and easier on the mouth—so it's best to try "Fetch my keys" after you've already taught your pet to "Take" some more obviously appealing objects. Try attaching a small treat bag containing one or two tiny edibles to your keyring; it'll make the keys immediately more attractive to him.

SAFETY If you have a young, excitable, and naturally "mouthy" dog, this may not be the best trick to teach him. You don't want him swallowing your car keys by accident! Use your common sense to decide whether this is a suitable trick for him.

▼ ONE Make sure that your dog watches you while you attach a small bag of treats to your keyring. Ask him to stand back while you place it on the floor. Then ask him to "Fetch it."

▲ TWO As he picks it up, call him to you, saying "Fetch my keys!" Use an excited voice; you don't want to give him too long to think about whether he's going to get the treats out by himself or bring the keys to you.

▼ THREE As he brings the keys, keep calling him and encouraging him—as soon as he reaches you, take the keys, praise him lavishly, and give him a treat. Practice this trick in between fetching easier things, so that he becomes accustomed to bringing you a range of different items.

Mind Games

How smart is your dog? She's your beloved pet, so you've always believed she's superintelligent, but have you ever tested her? The games and tricks in this section will encourage her to think for herself and to try to figure out what it is that you want her to do, too. Some will need to be learned in several stages, while others can be long-term projects—for example, there's no reason why, if she can learn the names for four items, she shouldn't go on to learn the names for a dozen or more. Now that you've worked your way through the basics, it's time to stretch her a little …

1, 2, 3, Treat!

There's an order to everything—and the trick here is to lay out some treats and ask your dog to collect them, working from the topmost of three steps down to the lowest one. A hungry dog may gobble up all the snacks before he's got the idea, so use small treats and have a few "Uh-uh" noises ready to let your dog know that he's not quite got it yet. If you teach this when he's already had a good run around, you may find that he's more able to focus.

TEACHING TIP

However hard you try, if you find that your dog gobbles down the treats without thinking about any "trick" element, change things around a little and teach your dog to "Follow the target" (see pages 70–71) using your finger, then move your hand down the stairs, corner to corner, asking your dog to "target" at each stop. If he's focused on you (and a reward when he's successful at doing what you ask), he may find it easier to pick up.

◀ ONE Lay out half a dozen treats down the lowest steps of a flight of stairs: one in each top corner of each step. Bring your dog to the stairs, point to the top step, indicating the treat on one side, and ask him to "Take it!" He won't need to be asked twice. Now indicate the second side of the step, and, as he eats the second treat, point to the third, on the step below.

SAFETY Don't ask a dog with back trouble to do this trick—backing down the stairs won't be good for his joints. Instead, lay out half a dozen treats on flat surfaces in a sequence, so that he can learn to take them in order, but without climbing up or down any steps.

◀ TWO He'll need to back down to the second step to get the second section of treats. Again, indicate the two different sides for him. Then encourage him to take the last treats offered.

▼ THREE As he gets the idea, you'll find that you'll be able to run to the stairs with him and dash through the treat sequence quickly. Eventually, he'll be picking them up for himself, in order, without any pauses, and in double-quick time.

Learn the Name

Your pet probably already understands a range of words—very few dogs don't recognize "dinner," "walk," and "bedtime," and many have far more words in their repertoire. The record is held by a border collie living in Germany that can identify well over 300 objects by name and, most impressively of all, can recognize them in pictures as well as in three-dimensional reality. Don't aim too high at first: Start by teaching your dog two favorite toys by name and asking her to pick up the one you indicate. Make sure she knows the "Take it" cue (see pages 44–45) before starting on "Learn the name."

▼ **ONE** Lay two familiar toys side by side on the floor. Don't start this game with a new toy—your dog may be too excited by the novelty of something fresh to play with to be able to concentrate on what you want her to do. Bring her into the room, walk over to the toys together and say "Take your tugger!" (or ball, Frisbee, etc) in an upbeat voice.

TEACHING TIP

If your dog is used to a clicker, it's particularly helpful with "Learn the name" and "Fetch the ..." (see pages 88–89) because you can click at the exact point at which she starts to go for the right toy and reinforce her decision—it's faster and more precise than a verbal reinforcement.

▶ TWO Your dog will probably recognize the "Take … " from "Take it"—and she'll want to pick up a toy because there's a chance of starting a game with you. If she goes straight for the toy you named, praise her and give her a treat right away. If she makes the other choice, say "Uh-uh!" and indicate the right one. Again, as soon as she takes it, praise her and give her a treat. Repeat a few times until she's going straight for the toy you name and picking it up.

▶ THREE Now repeat the whole process, but this time naming the second toy: "Take your ball!" She may get the idea right away, but if not, say "'Uh-uh!" when she makes the wrong choice. If she makes the wrong choice again and begins to get frustrated, hand her the right toy, repeating "Take your ball!" as you do, then praise her as soon as she has it in her mouth. Practice daily, varying which toy you name, and how often, until she always selects the right one of the two.

Fetch the ...

When your dog is confident playing "Learn the Name," extend his repertoire by adding different objects to his lineup. Most pets are able to learn up to a dozen different objects, provided that you stay patient and cheerful while you're teaching and you practice regularly. When he understands that he's being asked to make a selection (and this can be a surprisingly difficult concept for even smart dogs to grasp), then you can also try adding one unfamiliar object to the lineup and asking him to "Take the ...," simply using its unfamiliar name. Your dog may be able to deduce that you must be naming the unfamiliar object, because he knows the other names, and may also then select it to bring you. First things first, though: Here's how to start to enlarge his vocabulary.

◀ ONE Lay some toys on the floor. Pick two that you know that your dog can already identify, and two that you haven't yet taught him. Start by asking him to "Take" one of the familiar ones. When he gets it right, praise him and give him a treat.

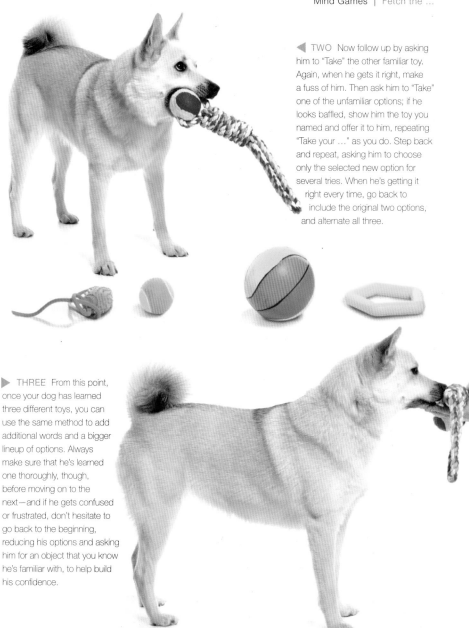

TWO Now follow up by asking him to "Take" the other familiar toy. Again, when he gets it right, make a fuss of him. Then ask him to "Take" one of the unfamiliar options; if he looks baffled, show him the toy you named and offer it to him, repeating "Take your …" as you do. Step back and repeat, asking him to choose only the selected new option for several tries. When he's getting it right every time, go back to include the original two options, and alternate all three.

THREE From this point, once your dog has learned three different toys, you can use the same method to add additional words and a bigger lineup of options. Always make sure that he's learned one thoroughly, though, before moving on to the next—and if he gets confused or frustrated, don't hesitate to go back to the beginning, reducing his options and asking him for an object that you know he's familiar with, to help build his confidence.

TWO She'll probably walk through the cones happily, but she may not immediately grasp the turn around each cone to make the complete figure-eight. Hold your hand/treat quite low and guide her clearly as she takes the turn after passing through the cones.

▲ ONE Arrange two small, light cones as shown (you can buy these in large sports or pet stores). If your dog is happy to follow a finger, use that as her guide; if she needs a bit more incentive, use a treat as a lure for the first few tries. Hold up the finger or treat alongside the first cone and say "Wind around!"

Wind Around

If your pet is a natural "spinner"—that's a dog who loves to run in circles and chase her tail when she's excited—you'll probably find that she's a natural for weaving routines. This is a mini version of the weaving trial on a real agility course. If she turns out to like walking a figure-eight shape, you can add a few more mini cones to extend her options—although you may have to move outdoors into the yard to extend her "course"!

BIG AND SMALL DOGS

Suit the distance between the cones to the size of your dog; the bigger the dog, the more space she'll need for her turns. As she becomes confident in her turns, you can move the cones slightly closer together to make the "weave" a little tougher.

▲ THREE Continue to guide her back through the gap and around the other cone. Repeat "Wind around!" if you need to, and if she doesn't seem to get the idea right away, you can walk just ahead of her and take the turns yourself, too.

▶ FOUR As she completes the figure-eight, praise her and give her a treat. Take another couple of turns. Eventually, she should be happy to make the turns on only a verbal cue.

91

Cone Ball

This game is a variation of a simple "Fetch." It will appeal strongly to any dog who is a ball enthusiast. When he's learned the basic version, you can place two or three cones, each topped by a tennis ball, in the yard and ask him to bring you one before you play a "Fetch" game with him. That way, he'll get plenty of exercise. See if he can identify which ball to fetch if you point to the cone you want—some dogs seem to recognize the intention of "their" humans pointing with a finger, while others appear completely baffled by it!

SMALL DOGS

If your dog is too little to reach a ball on even the smallest cone, improvise. You can balance a ball on an upturned plastic bowl, or any other accessible object. Don't ask a tiny dog to jump for "Cone Ball"—the cone isn't stable enough for him to brace himself on.

▼ ONE Set up a small, light cone with a tennis ball balanced on top of it. (If your dog is magnetically drawn to any tennis ball he sees, it's best to do this out of sight). Call him to you and ask him to "Fetch the ball." If he doesn't seem to get the idea immediately, run over to the cone with him and indicate the ball with your hand.

◀ TWO As he moves to pick the ball up from the cone, praise him. As soon as he has it in his mouth, call him to you, making a lot of enthusiastic noise.

▶ THREE When he reaches you, hold out your hand and ask him to give you the ball. If he's not immediately willing to give it up, take it from his mouth (gently—don't encourage him to think that you're playing tug with him). If he loves fetch games, throw it for him as a reward.

ACHOO!!!

▲ ONE Place a tissue box on a low, stable surface. Pull a tissue halfway out of it, and practice by saying "Take it! Achoo!" while showing it to your dog. When she's happy to pull a tissue from the box (and this is probably the hardest part of the trick, so practice patiently until she's got it out), back off a step or two and repeat "Take it! Achoo!" Your dog will take the cue to collect the tissue.

Caught a Cold

This is a great trick to show off when you have company. Cued by a loud, theatrical sneeze, your dog will run off to collect you a tissue from the box handily situated on a low surface nearby and run back to you with it firmly held in her mouth. True, it's likely to be a bit damp and squishy by the time it's "handed" to you, but no matter, this is so cute that it always wins a big round of applause. Practice it until she gets it perfect every time before you show off to your friends. Learn the trick stage by stage; it's quite complex, so be prepared for short, frequent sessions while you're teaching it.

TEACHING TIP

Some dogs seem to steady the tissue box with a paw naturally. However, if your pet knocks the box over and finds it hard to angle, use duct tape to stick it to the surface you've placed it on; she'll find it easier if all she has to do is focus on pulling out the tissue.

TWO Praise her enthusiastically as she heads for the tissue box. At this point, she may be ready to pull the tissue out on her own, or she may need some help with a verbal cue.

THREE Make sure that the tissue is pulled out of the box to the point where it's very easy for her to remove it. Give her plenty of encouragement as she pulls. As soon as she's got it free of the box, call her back to you.

FOUR When she brings the tissue over, praise her lavishly and take the tissue (if she's reluctant to let it go, you can keep a treat concealed in your hand and engineer a neat swap with her).

ONE Make a gift using several layers of thick paper and a prize in the center—a dog treat, or a squeaky toy if your dog loves things that make a noise, should be enough incentive for him to play. Show it to him—wave it around a little if you need to so you have his interest, then tear through one layer at a corner of the gift and hand it to him.

▲ TWO Encourage him to tear through a layer of paper and pull the smaller gift out. Try not to let him tear right through the gift at the first attempt (see box on right), or it will be a very short game. Just as he reaches the second layer, take the gift gently from him, saying "Give me!" as you do. Praise him warmly as soon as he gives it up to you.

Pass the Gift

Any dog can unwrap a gift if he can sniff a tasty treat inside, but what about if there are several layers? It takes a bright dog to learn how to undo one layer, hand the gift back to you, and then take it back again for his next turn. Teach this trick with plenty of rewards along the way, or the downcast expression of your dog as he hands back a gift that he knows has something delicious inside may discourage you from practicing until he has it perfect.

THREE Let him watch as you tear a layer of paper off the gift yourself, then hand it back to him, saying "Go ahead!"

FOUR You might not manage more than one handover the first few times you play this game; your dog will get so excited that he'll tear to the center the second time you hand him the gift. Try to control his excitement with your tone of voice—low and quiet—when you're giving the verbal cues; with time, he'll learn enough restraint to cope with two or three handovers before he goes for the prize.

TEACHING TIP

We wrapped the gift in plenty of varied and colorful wrapping paper to show the layers clearly for the photography. However, you don't have to use special paper for your own version—your dog won't care if it's plain brown paper and layers of newspaper, as long as he's enjoying the game! Either wrap in thick layers or use heavy paper to ensure that he doesn't just tear straight through to the treat the moment he starts to use his teeth.

How Many Fingers?

Can your dog really count? Probably not, but you can make it look as if she can by asking her to bark the number of fingers you're holding up. Timing is absolutely crucial for this trick—you need to let her know not only exactly when to start barking but also just when to stop. And it's demanding for her, because she must learn from both verbal and visual signals (eventually, you'll be dropping the verbal ones). Be patient—unless your dog is one of the few who is really averse to barking, she'll get it in the end. The more fingers you start with holding up, the more time you're giving yourself to get her to stop on cue.

▼ ONE If your dog already barks on demand (for example "Answer the door" on pages 36–37), then you can use this to start the "counting." If not, encourage her to bark with an exciting noise, using the verbal cue "Count!" and holding up one hand with the fingers spread out. It may take a while to teach, but don't move on to the second step until she is barking on cue to the verbal and visual signal.

▼ TWO Now teach her to stop the barking. As she begins, keep your hand held up for a moment or two, but after three or four barks use your other hand to give a "stop" signal (hand down and palm in), saying "Stop!" in a low, calm voice as you do. Again, she'll eventually get the idea with plenty of practice. Be ready to praise her and give her a treat as soon as she stops.

▶ THREE As your dog becomes used to the visual cues, you can gradually abandon the verbal ones until she is barking and stopping purely on hand signals. Practice holding up four fingers, say, on your "barking" hand, and stopping her barking exactly after four barks. Try a short practice every day until you both have your timings accurate—eventually you'll be able to reduce the number of fingers first to three and then two, increasing the number of options for her to bark as "answers."

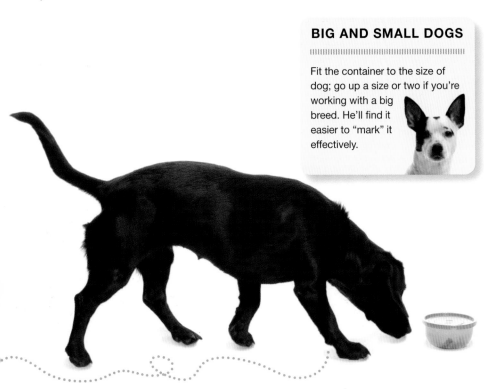

Mark It

An untrained pet, shown a box with a treat in it, will usually use both paws and mouth to try to open the box to get at the treat. In "Mark it," you're showing him how to lightly mark the box with his paw—as soon as he gets it right, he'll be given the treat as a reward. You'll need a small, light container with a tight-fitting lid and a really good food treat for this game. Cut a small hole or slit in the top of the container before you start so that your pet can smell the delicious morsel of sausage or cheese you've hidden inside.

▲ ONE Show your pet the box and let him sniff around it before you put any food inside. Then put the treat in while he isn't watching, close the lid, place it on the floor, and call him in. He'll go straight for the box and start to sniff at it.

▼ TWO As soon as he's figured out that the treat is closed inside, he'll try to use both his mouth and paws to get the lid off. Don't let him do this for more than a second or two; instead, quickly step in, take one of his front paws, and tap it lightly on the box, saying "Mark it!" as you do. If you use a clicker to teach, the exact moment that his paw touches the box lid is the time to click. Sit back, repeat "Mark it!" and see if he's made the connection between paw and cue. You may need to repeat it a few times before he understands that it's the paw movement that you want from him.

▶ THREE The moment he places a paw on the box of his own accord, take the lid off the box and give him the treat. At first you may need to reward a good attempt—say, a paw movement toward the box. However, as he becomes used to the game, aim for a clear paw tap every time before you treat him.

Show Me

In "Mark it," you taught your dog to show you where the treat is by putting her paw on the container; in this follow-up, you're going to ask her to choose from three options. As she already knows the cue that gets her the treat, adding to the number of boxes shouldn't hold her up for long, although she'll probably have to give them all a thorough sniff before making her selection. When she's used to playing, try some variants by putting treats in every box (she'll wonder which to mark first) or in two out of the three containers you've lined up. Offering her an unexpected option (and the possibility of an extra treat or two) will keep her enthusiastic about the game.

▼ ONE Start by laying out three lidded containers of about the same size, each with a small slit cut in the top. Put a treat in one box, bring your dog in, and ask her to "Mark it." She may have to sniff all three, but she'll readily identify which box has the treat in and mark it with her paw. Praise her and give her a treat—but now make things more complex.

▶ TWO Put tiny treats in two boxes and a larger one in the third. Line them up, call your dog in, and ask her to "Mark it"—which does she pick? Open whichever box she marks, give her what's inside, then ask her to mark another. When you've been through all three boxes, repeat the sequence and see if she goes for the big treat first.

▼ THREE Try playing favorites—different kinds of treats in each box. Can she pick out her favorite? This game is fun for you because you're kept guessing about your dog's choices, and it's fun for her because it puts her in a no-lose situation—whichever container she goes for, there's at least one treat to be had.

The Hard Stuff

You and your pet have worked through a few tricks together, so now it's time for the hard stuff. Of course, there have already been some options that called on the two of you to practice a lot in the previous sections, but this chapter offers a range of challenging extras. Follow the rules to ensure that your dog still has fun: make sure you're consistent when you teach, keep the lessons short and upbeat, and always, always stop or change things around if he's getting bored or frustrated by a game. An interested dog is a happy dog—and it's your job to ensure he stays engaged with you while he's learning.

▲ ONE Take a plastic target (it's a round, plastic disk; you can buy them in pet stores, or use the plastic top from a tube of tennis balls or potato chips) and a blob of poster putty. Start by sticking the target somewhere easy and accessible—you could just lay it on the floor. Then call your dog.

Touch the Spot

Identifying and "marking" a target wherever it's placed is a great start to some advanced learning (it's the main building block to teaching your dog to direct her strength and can be used to teach her to open a door, for example—see pages 110–111). Dogs vary on which part of them they choose to "mark" with—one dog may prefer to use her nose, another her paw. Concentrate on asking her to mark or push the target with her paw, because it will carry more of her body weight behind it when you want to direct her strength to a specific task.

SAFETY **Always place the target on a stable surface for your pet; if she jumps to mark it and whatever you've secured it to slips and slithers about, she may become reluctant to touch it again.**

▶ TWO Point to the target. As she goes to investigate, wait to see if she touches it with her nose or paw. If you use a clicker, click the second her paw touches the target, saying "Touch!" and give her a treat. Otherwise, wait for the right moment, but say "Touch!" and give her a treat in the same way. If she doesn't immediately make the connection, you can sit alongside the target and tap it with your finger or even gently place her paw on it, then give her the chance to do it for herself and praise her as soon as she gets it right.

▼ THREE As soon as she's regularly going straight for the target, move it around onto some different surfaces, such as a wall, a piece of furniture, or even a person. She'll soon understand that, wherever the target is placed, "Touch" is asking her to touch it with a paw.

Shut the Door

▲ ONE Before you start "Shut the door" make sure that your pet has completely mastered "Touch the spot" (see pages 106–107). When he's confidently touching the target every time, place it at his natural paw height on a closed door (something like a kitchen cabinet is ideal) and ask him to touch it.

You're settled on the couch watching television when someone comes into the room and forgets to shut the door. How impressive if you can call to your dog and ask him to close the door for you! And your dog will love the laughter and praise when he does it successfully in front of company. Practice it thoroughly before you show it off, and when you're sure he'll do it when asked, keep your tone casual ("Casey, could you shut the door?") so that onlookers are even more surprised when he trots over on cue and pushes it closed.

SAFETY While your dog is learning this trick, it's best to hold the door yourself to make sure that it closes in a controlled way and doesn't fly shut, causing him to lose his balance. Even when he's learned it, ask him to shut only familiar doors that won't slam shut or be too heavy for him to push.

◀ TWO When you've practiced a few times, move the target up, little by little, until he's standing and pushing the target at a height at which most of his body weight will be placed against the door.

▶ THREE Finally, ask him to "Touch" a target placed high on a door that is slightly ajar. Hold it at the top so that it will close slowly as he pushes. Practice on one or two familiar doors, leaving them a little more open every time, and start to add "Shut the door" as he jumps and pushes. Eventually, when he's used to jumping, pushing, and balancing in a single sequence, you'll be able to remove the target altogether and ask him to "Shut the door" for himself. Be generous with rewards while he's still learning; this is quite a tough trick, so you'll need to keep him motivated.

SAFETY If you're teaching your dog to open doors, make sure that she won't come across anything dangerous with her newfound ability. Don't forget that lots of everyday household cleaning materials, for example, can be harmful to dogs, so if you teach her to open a cupboard, only that cupboard door should have a tug on it, and only safe treats or toys should be kept inside.

Open the Door

Just as impressive as "Shut the door," this trick is usually considerably easier to teach. Dogs can't get a grip on most door handles, but if you tie a tug to the handle you want your dog to open, she'll get the idea quickly. Eventually, she may even be able to let herself out into the yard—but don't forget to teach her to close the door after herself!

▲ ONE Before you start, play a game of tug-of-war with your dog. Ideally, play with the rope or fabric you'll eventually be tying to the door handle so that your pet associates it with pulling (and games). When you play with her, say "Pull!" as she tugs at her end to help her connect the action with the word. After the game, loop the rope around handle of the door you want her to open and hand it to her, saying "Pull!"

◄ TWO If she hesitates to take it in her mouth, pull on it a little yourself until she shows some interest, and then offer it to her again.

▼ THREE Once she has it in her mouth, she'll start to pull. As she pulls, keep a hand on top of the door so that it doesn't fly open and scare her. When the door starts to open, say "Open the door!" and giver her praise and a treat. Gradually, as she becomes more confident, you'll be able to drop the "Pull" cue and eventually simply send her to "Open the door" by herself.

▼ ONE To "fetch his snack" effectively, your pet needs first to have learned the steps to "Open the door" on pages 110–111. When he confidently opens the door every time without needing your help, prepare a treat for him (make it something that you know he really loves and that will take a little time to eat) and place it inside the cabinet.

SMALL DOGS

This trick will work just as well for small dogs, but make sure the door he's expected to open to get to the snack isn't too heavy for him, and that the treat inside is portable once he has. A light cabinet door with a tug pull at a reachable level and a treat on the floor inside will work best for a little dog.

Fetch Your Snack

When you've taught your dog to open a cabinet door, it's great if he finds something worthwhile inside. This is a good party piece—you can wait until your guests are settling down for a meal around your table, then send your pet to collect his own snack so that you can all eat together. Something like an appropriately sized stuffed Nylabone toy will be a worthwhile snack for your dog to collect.

▼ TWO Accompany him to the cabinet and ask him to "Open the door." When he's opened it, point to the rawhide chew, stuffed Nylabone, or whatever other delicacy you've laid in an accessible place inside and say "Fetch your snack!" He won't usually need much encouragement, but make sure it's placed so that he can reach it easily and pick it up in his mouth. If he seems uncertain whether he can just take it, repeat "Fetch your snack!" enthusiastically, picking it up and handing it to him at the same time.

▼ THREE If you practice regularly, your dog will gradually learn "Fetch your snack" as a cue of its own, and you'll be able to dispense with the "Open the door" cue. If you'd like a little regular downtime with your dog, you could even turn "Fetch your snack" into a daily ritual, factoring in ten minutes' peace and quiet for you while he enjoys his treat.

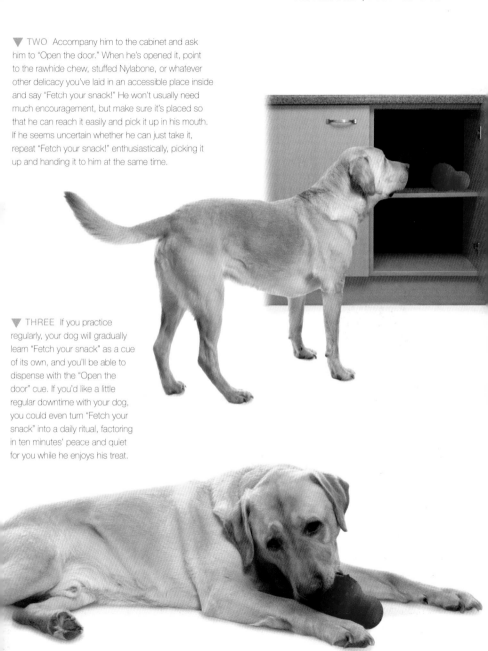

"Over" — Hurdling

I f your dog is already eager to jump, hurdling won't take much teaching. A little routine in which she first leaps over the jump and then returns to wriggle under it is a bit more complicated. Keep the noises you make for over the jump and under the jump very different—a high-pitched "hup" together with an "up" gesture of your hand will encourage her to jump over. You can make a jump—indoors or outdoors—with a broom handle placed across two cones of a suitable height. Make sure that the pole rolls off easily so that she won't hurt herself if she miscalculates on takeoff.

▲ ONE Even if your dog jumps onto the couch or leaps low obstacles outdoors when she's playing, she may be a little more doubtful about jumping over a hurdle. Whether you set it up inside or outside, make sure that there's enough space for her to take a small run up to it, and start with it set very low—you can raise the bar when she's confident about tackling it. Ask her to sit on one side of the jump as you stand at the other, show her a treat as a lure, and lift it up and away, over the jump, saying "Hup!" as you do so.

▼ **TWO** She may jump right away. If not, try walking up to the jump with her and even taking a run and jumping yourself. Take it a few more times until she's jumping without hesitation. If the bar is very low, try raising it a little at a time. Now it's time for the limbo …

SAFETY Jumping needs to be taken in careful stages. Elderly or arthritic dogs shouldn't be encouraged to jump too much, or, if they are really stiff, at all. If you're not sure whether a dog will be happy jumping, watch her everyday behavior; if she jumps naturally while she's playing or jumps on or off furniture, teaching her to jump on demand will be fine.

And "Under" — Limbo

Once your dog has learned to go over a jump, try showing him how to go under it. Just as a jump shouldn't be placed too high at first, so a limbo pole (which the jump now becomes) shouldn't be placed too low. When you're setting up, place the pole low enough for your dog to have to crouch a little, but not so low that she has to go straight into a flat-belly crawl. Practice a few times before trying to take it a little lower.

▼ ONE Place the pole at an appropriate height and show your dog a treat. Hold it low, with your hand very close to the ground. Your dog will stretch to reach it.

SAFETY Just as with jumping, crawling shouldn't be encouraged if your dog is old, stiff, or has a bad back or hips. Use your judgment about whether this is a suitable game for him, but if you've decided to try it and he shows any discomfort at all, stop right away.

▶ TWO Pull the treat forward slightly, so that it's a little farther from your dog's nose. He'll naturally go down to stretch to reach it and so will begin to move under the pole. Keep it just out of his reach, saying "Limbo!" encouragingly as he moves.

▼ THREE As soon as he's successfully under the pole, praise your dog and give him a treat. Take two or three more practice runs, then, if he seems to be doing the limbo very easily, lower the pole a little. Don't lower it beyond the point at which he's in a flat crawl—that's low enough. Now try asking your dog alternately to jump over and limbo under the pole.

Laundry Service

Many dogs, particularly "mouthy" breeds, such as spaniels and retrievers, love to carry soft fabric items in their mouths. If your dog already knows "Take it," why not turn her natural inclination into a useful trick and teach her to collect the laundry for you? The hardest part may be getting your dog to let go of the things she's taken and to place them in the laundry basket; most dogs enjoy the collecting part the most, but will quickly learn to trade a treat for a sock or T-shirt.

▼ ONE Put a pile of laundry items on the floor on one side of the room and place the basket across the room from them. Pick up a sock and hand it to your dog, asking her to "Take it."

SAFETY Surprising numbers of dogs are taken to the veterinarian each year to have socks or other small items of clothing surgically removed from their stomachs. Don't encourage your dog to "mouth" on small items of laundry when you're not playing this game— if she loves to carry something soft around with her, buy her a custom-made, large, soft dog toy instead.

TWO Have a treat ready and, as she takes the sock in her mouth, run over to the laundry basket with her (show her the treat to lure her if she needs encouragement).

THREE When she's holding her laundry right over the basket, hold your hand out with the treat and, as she drops the sock into the basket, say "Laundry service!" and give her the treat. Run back to the laundry pile with her and choose another piece for her to collect. She'll quickly get the idea that she can swap laundry for a treat and will start to bring the pieces over for herself. As she gets familiar with the game, treat her for only every second or third piece of laundry. Eventually, just the "Laundry service" cue will be enough to get her gathering up the laundry!

Freeze

Some children play a game in which a child tries to sneak up behind the "person" as quietly as he or she can, and has to freeze in position when the person turns around. Well, this is a version for you and your pet to play. Not all dogs take to it, but even if you end up romping together as he fails to "freeze" at the right moment, you'll both have a lot of fun. Ask a human friend to play alongside your dog to help him to get the idea of stopping and starting; he'll find it easier if he has someone creeping and freezing alongside him.

▼ ONE Have your friend and your dog stand a little distance from you, across the room (or the yard if you're playing outside). Turn your back to them. Ask your friend to move toward you very, very slowly and quietly. She can encourage your dog to move alongside her (a good cue for slow-and-quiet with dogs is a finger held to the lips) equally slowly and quietly. If she exaggerates how stealthily she's moving, he's likely to copy her.

▶ TWO When they're still some distance behind you, turn around slowly. Your friend will immediately "freeze" in position, staying absolutely still. If your dog looks as though he's about to leap toward you, say "Sta-a-a-ay!," drawing out the word in a low, soothing voice. Then turn your back again.

▼ THREE Gesturing to your pet, your friend will begin to move forward slowly again. This time, let her get all the way to you and "catch" you before you turn around. Make a fuss of both dog and friend. Don't try more than two "freezes" for the first few times you practice this game; your dog will probably get too excited and burst into activity if you ramp the tension too high. If he suddenly loses control and rushes over to you at the wrong moment, say "Uh-uh!" and ask him to go back in place.

Push the Ball

Some dogs are as fascinated by ball play as the most eager human soccer fan. If you have a dog who's an enthusiast, practice with her regularly to teach her how to push the ball with her nose, "head" it when it's in the air, and run along, directing the ball with a mix of chasing and dribbling it, while maintaining perfect "paw" control. If she can learn all this, you can play mixed dog/human ball games that will be enjoyable for both parties, and wonderful exercise for both you and your pet. Start by teaching her to push the ball.

SAFETY Choose the ball your dog plays with carefully. It should be a good weight and size—not too heavy for her to be able to push easily or "head," and not so light that she simply picks it up rather than pushing it. A foam-filled, hard, pet ball of an appropriate size is a good choice; she won't deflate it if she accidentally sinks her teeth in.

▶ ONE Place the ball on the floor with a treat just underneath it. Call your dog over, and she'll push her nose under the ball to get at the treat. As she noses it and the ball moves, say "Push!" Repeat two or three times, saying "Push!" every time she noses at the ball.

▶ TWO After a couple of sessions of practice, try asking her to "Push" without placing a treat under the ball. For some dogs, the rolling ball is exciting enough without any inducements, but if she doesn't start to nose and push the ball right away, roll it toward her and ask her to "Push" it back to you. Turn the interaction into a game and offer her a treat when she returns it to you.

▲ THREE As she gets used to pushing the ball around you can gently kick it toward her, skirt around her while she's dribbling it, and generally encourage her to join in with you playing with the ball rather than keeping it all to herself.

▶ ONE Start by playing a game of "Push the ball" (see pages 122–123) so that he's enthusiastic about the ball before you start. Then ask him to sit, hold the ball up in both hands, and throw it gently toward him, saying "Push!" as you do.

Head the Ball

I f you've already taught your dog to push the ball, the next step is encouraging him to head it into the air. Make sure the ball you choose isn't too heavy or cumbersome—dogs can get excited in the middle of a game, so it's important that he can't hurt himself. Once he's learned to head the ball, you'll be able to teach him to score a goal or head it over a net, depending on your own favorite game.

▼ TWO He may immediately
try to jump and push the ball. If he
doesn't, have another try. Keep
saying "Push!" whenever you
throw, and as soon as he tries to
nose it midair, praise him and give
him a treat, even if he doesn't
immediately succeed.

▶ THREE Don't expect your pet to learn to head the
ball efficiently in just a couple of sessions. Practice little
and often and alternate throwing and rolling the ball, so
that he gets the opportunity both to head it and to dribble
it. Wait until he's completely confident with "heading" a
thrown ball before you introduce other players (human or
canine) to the game.

Index

Acknowledgments

They say you should never work with animals or children. The Ivy Press would like to thank Nick Ridley for his skill and good humor in photographing the dogs, and all at Hearing Dogs for Deaf People (www.hearingdogs.org.uk) for their help. Particular thanks go to Millie Smith for her forward planning, lateral thinking, and superhuman patience during the photo sessions. We were grateful, too, to all the dog handlers and owners who helped and, of course, to all the dogs, who couldn't have been more fun to work with. They triumphantly disproved the truism about working with animals. The jury is still out on children.

Cedar   Joey   Toby   Chutney   Bruce

Bertie   Scout   JD   Mojo   Tean

Benni   Mr. Flynn   Byron   Juicie   Brodick

Busta   Whisper   Max